The Wisdom of the East

EDITED BY J. L. CRANMER-BYNG M.C.

A LUTE OF JADE

By the same author

A FEAST OF LANTERNS
ODES TO CONFUCIUS
THE ROSE GARDEN OF SA'DI

Sole distributors in the USA
PARAGON BOOK GALLERY INC.,
Booksellers and Publishers
NEW YORK · NY · USA

A LUTE OF JADE

Selections from the Classical Poets of China

RENDERED
WITH AN INTRODUCTION BY

L. Cranmer-Byng

With lutes of gold and lutes of jade
Li Po

JOHN MURRAY
50 Albemarle Street
LONDON

First published 1909
Second edition 1911
Reprinted 1913
Reprinted 1915
Reprinted 1917
Reprinted 1918
Reprinted 1926
Reprinted 1936
Reprinted 1944
Reprinted 1959

Printed in Great Britain
by Butler & Tanner Ltd
Frome and London

To
Professor Herbert Giles

The object of the Editor of this series is a very definite one. He desires above all things that these books shall be the ambassadors of good-will between East and West. He hopes that they will contribute to a fuller knowledge of the great cultural heritage of the East, for only through real understanding will the West be able to appreciate the underlying problems and aspirations of Asia to-day. He is confident that a deeper knowledge of the great ideals and lofty philosophy of Eastern thought will help to a revival of that true spirit of charity which neither despises nor fears the nations of another creed and colour.

J. L. CRANMER-BYNG

50 *Albemarle Street*
  London, W.1

Contents

Contents

Contents

Preface

The continuing appeal of this book since it was first published in 1909 is proof of a certain quality in my father's renderings which is not easy to define. He purposely called them 'renderings' for he was careful not to claim them as translations in the accepted sense of the word. Knowing no Chinese himself, my father based these poems on literal translations made by his friend Herbert Giles, who was Professor of Chinese at Cambridge University from 1897 to 1932, and to whom this book is dedicated. The partnership was an immediate success and I am happy to know that one of those who turned to *A Lute of Jade* with continual enjoyment was Thomas Hardy.

The translation of Chinese poetry presents many problems and requires outstanding ability in the use of the English language. Due to the conciseness of Chinese a literal version cannot be as expansive as we would like, since the Chinese language is already cut to the bone and a literal translation becomes a mere telegram. Furthermore the Chinese sense of rhyme is delicate, and whereas in their rhyme-schemes they use words that to our ears sound like homophones, to Chinese ears they bring a subtle inner music. Yet this creates another difficulty, for the use of a similar rhyme-scheme in English, unless in the hands of a writer of unusual skill, produces a dreary sing-song. In recent years translators have shied away from the use of rhyme for this reason, but there are now signs of its coming back into favour.

A Lute of Jade, however, is free from such controversy, for these poems exist in their own right, following an English pattern. Yet their content is sufficiently close to that of the originals to give something of the flavour of each poet and to show something of his style. Perhaps in this sense my father was more successful than those who transcribe the literal meaning of Chinese poetry. For he strove to grasp the essence of the original poem and then to transmute it through his own understanding of Chinese culture until it lived again as an English poem. Perhaps it is this quality which has kept these poems fresh for over fifty years.

J. L. C-B.

Introduction

The Ancient Ballads

A little under three hundred years, from A.D. 618 to 906, the period of the T'ang dynasty, and the great age of Chinese poetry had come and gone. Far back in the twilight of history, at least 1,700 years before Christ, the Chinese people sang their songs of kings and feudal princes good or bad, of husbandry, or now and then songs with the more personal note of simple joys and sorrows. All things in these Odes collected by Confucius belong to the surface of life; they are the work of those who easily plough light furrows, knowing nothing of hidden gold. Only at rare moments of exaltation or despair do we hear the lyrical cry rising above the monotone of dreamlike content. Even the magnificent outburst at the beginning of this book, in which the unhappy woman compares her heart to a dying moon, is prefaced by vague complaint:

> My brothers, although they support me not,
> Are angry if I speak of my sadness.
>
> My sadness is so great,
> Nearly all are jealous of me;
> Many calumnies attack me,

> And scorning spares me not.
> Yet what harm have I done?
> I can show a clear conscience.

Yes, the conscience is clear and the song is clear, and so these little streams flow on, shining in the clear dawn of a golden past to which all poets and philosophers to come will turn with wistful eyes. These early ballads of the Chinese differ in feeling from almost all the ballad literature of the world. They are ballads of peace, while those of other nations are so often war-songs and the remembrances of brave deeds. Many of them are sung to a refrain. More especially is this the case with those whose lines breathe sadness, where the refrain comes like a sigh at the end of a regret:

> Cold from the spring the waters pass
> Over the waving pampas grass,
>   All night long in dream I lie,
>   Ah me! ah me! to awake and sigh—
>   Sigh for the City of Chow.

> Cold from its source the stream meanders
> Darkly down through the oleanders,
>   All night long in dream I lie,
>   Ah me! ah me! to awake and sigh—
>   Sigh for the City of Chow.

In another place the refrain urges and importunes; it is time for flight:

> Cold and keen the north wind blows,
> Silent falls the shroud of snows.
> You who gave me your heart,
> Let me join hands and depart!

Is this a time for delay?
Now, while we may,
· Let us away.

Only the lonely fox is red,
Black but the crow-flight overhead
You who gave me your heart—
The chariot creaks to depart.
Is this a time for delay?
Now, while we may,
Let us away.

Perhaps these Odes may best be compared with the little craftless figures in an early age of pottery, when the fragrance of the soil yet lingered about the rough clay. The maker of the song was a poet, and knew it not. The maker of the bowl was an artist, and knew it not. You will get no finish from either—the lines are often blurred, the design but half fulfilled; and yet the effect is not inartistic. It has been well said that greatness is but another name for interpretation; and in so far as these nameless workmen of old interpreted themselves and the times in which they lived, they have attained enduring greatness.

POETRY BEFORE THE T'ANGS

Following on the Odes, we have much written in the same style, more often than not by women, or songs possibly written to be sung by them, always in a minor key, fraught with sadness, yet full of quiet resignation and pathos.

Introduction

It is necessary to mention in passing the celebrated Ch'ü Yüan (fourth century B.C.), minister and kinsman of a petty kinglet under the Chou dynasty, whose *Li Sao*, literally translated *Falling into Trouble*, is partly autobiography and partly imagination. His death by drowning gave rise to the great Dragon-boat Festival, which was originally a solemn annual search for the body of the poet.

Soon a great national dynasty arrives whose Emperors are often patrons of literature and occasionally poets as well. The House of Han (200 B.C.–A.D. 200) has left its mark upon the Empire of China, whose people of to-day still call themselves 'Sons of Han'. There were Emperors beloved of literary men, Emperors beloved of the people, builders of long waterways and glittering palaces, and one great conqueror, the Emperor Wu Ti, of almost legendary fame. This was an age of preparation and development of new forces. Under the Hans, Buddhism first began to flourish. The effect is seen in the poetry of the time, especially towards the closing years of this dynasty. The minds of poets sought refuge in the ideal world from the illusions of the senses.

The third century A.D. saw the birth of what was probably the first literary club ever known, the Seven Sages of the Bamboo Grove. This little coterie of friends was composed of seven famous men, who possessed many talents in common, being poets and musicians, alchemists, philosophers, and mostly hard drinkers as well. Their poetry, however, is scarcely memorable. Only one great name stands between them and the poets of the T'ang dynasty—the name of T'ao Ch'ien (A.D. 365–427), whose exquisite allegory 'The Peach Blossom Fountain' is quoted by Professor Giles in his *Chinese Literature*. The philosophy of this ancient poet appears to have been that of Horace. *Carpe diem!*

'Ah, how short a time it is that we are here! Why then not set our hearts at rest, ceasing to trouble whether we remain or go? What boots it to wear out the soul with anxious thoughts? I want not wealth; I want not power; heaven is beyond my hopes. Then let me stroll through the bright hours as they pass, in my garden among my flowers, or I will mount the hill and sing my song, or weave my verse beside the limpid brook. Thus will I work out my allotted span, content with the appointments of Fate, my spirit free from care.' [1] For him enjoyment and scarcely happiness is the thing. And although many of his word-pictures are not lacking in charm or colour, they have but little significance beyond them. They are essentially the art works of an older school than that of the Seven Sages. But we must have due regard for them, for they only miss greatness by a little, and remind us of the faint threnodies that stir in the throats of bird musicians upon the dawn.

[1] Giles, *Chinese Literature*, p. 130.

Introduction

THE POETS OF THE T'ANG DYNASTY

At last the golden age of Chinese poetry is at hand.
Call the roll of these three hundred eventful years, and
all the great masters of song will answer you. This is an
age of professional poets, whom emperors and statesmen delight to honour. With the Chinese, verse-
making has always been a second nature. It is one of
the accomplishments which no man of education would
be found lacking. Colonel Cheng-Ki-Tong, in his
delightful book *The Chinese Painted by Themselves*, says:
'Poetry has been in China, as in Greece, the language
of the gods. It was poetry that inculcated laws and
maxims; it was by the harmony of its lines that tradi-
tions were handed down at a time when memory had
to supply the place of writing; and it was the first
language of wisdom and of inspiration.' It has been
above all the recreation of statesmen and great officials,
a means of escape from the weariness of public life and
the burden of ruling. A study of the interminable
biographies of Chinese poets and men of letters would
reveal but a few professional poets, men whose lives
were wholly devoted to their art; and of these few the
T'ang dynasty can claim nearly all. Yet strange as it
may seem, this matters but little when the quality of
Chinese poetry is considered. The great men of the age
were at once servants of duty and the lords of life. To
them official routine and the responsibilities of the
state were burdens to be borne along the highway,
with periods of rest and intimate reunion with nature

to cheer the travellers. When the heavy load was laid aside, song rose naturally from the lips. Subtly connecting the arts, they were at once painters and poets, musicians and singers. And because they were philosophers and seekers after the beauty that underlies the form of things, they made the picture express its own significance, and every song find echo in the souls of those that heard. You will find no tedium of repetition in all their poetry, no thin vein of thought beaten out over endless pages. The following extract from an ancient treatise on the art of poetry called *Ming-Chung* sets forth most clearly certain ideals to be pursued:

'To make a good poem, the subject must be interesting, and treated in an attractive manner; genius must shine throughout the whole, and be supported by a graceful, brilliant, and sublime style. The poet ought to traverse, with a rapid flight, the lofty regions of philosophy, without deviating from the narrow way of truth. . . . Good taste will only pardon such digressions as bring him towards his end, and show it from a most striking point of view.

'Disappointment must attend him, if he speaks without speaking to the purpose, or without describing things with that fire, with that force, and with that energy which present them to the mind as a painting does to the eyes. Bold thought, untiring imagination, softness and harmony, make a true poem.

'One must begin with grandeur, paint everything expressed, soften the shades of those which are of least importance, collect all into one point of view, and carry the reader thither with a rapid flight.'

Yet when due respect has been paid to this critic of old time, the fact still remains that concentration and suggestion are the two essentials of Chinese poetry. There is neither Iliad nor Odyssey to be found in the libraries of the Chinese; indeed, a favourite feature of their verse is the 'stop short', a poem containing only four lines, concerning which another critic has explained that only the words stop, while the sense goes on. But what a world of meaning is to be found between four short lines! Often a door is opened, a curtain drawn aside, in the halls of romance, where the reader may roam at will. With this nation of artists in emotion, the taste of the tea is a thing of lesser importance; it is the aroma which remains and delights. The poems of the T'angs are full of this subtle aroma, this suggestive compelling fragrance which lingers when the songs have passed away. It is as though the Æolian harps had caught some strayed wind from an unknown world, and brought strange messages from peopled stars.

A deep simplicity touching many hidden springs, a profound regard for the noble uses of leisure, things which modern critics of life have taught us to despise— these are the technique and the composition and colour of all their work.

Complete surrender to a particular mood until the mood itself surrenders to the artist, and afterwards silent ceaseless toil until a form worthy of its expression has been achieved—this is the method of Li Po and his fellows. And as for leisure, it means life with all its possibilities of beauty and romance. The artist is ever saying, 'Stay a little while! See, I have captured one moment from eternity.' Yet it is only in the East that poetry is truly appreciated, by those to whom leisure to look around them is vital as the air they breathe. This explains the welcome given by Chinese Emperors and Caliphs of Bagdad to all roving minstrels in whose immortality, like flies in amber, they are caught.

A POET'S EMPEROR

In the long list of imperial patrons the name of the Emperor Ming Huang of the T'ang dynasty holds the foremost place. History alone would not have immortalized his memory.[1] But romance is nearer to this Emperor's life than history. He was not a great ruler, but an artist stifled in ceremony and lost in statecraft. Yet what Emperor could escape immortality who had Tu Fu and Li Po for contemporaries, Ch'ang-an for his capital, and T'ai Chên of a thousand songs to wife? Poet and sportsman, mystic and man of this world, a great polo player, and the passionate lover of one beautiful woman whose ill-starred fate inspired Po Chü-i, the tenderest of all their singers,[2] Ming Huang is more to literature than to history. Of his life and

[1] A.D. 685–762.   [2] See p. 72.

times the poets are faithful recorders. Tu Fu in *The Old Man of Shao-Ling* leaves us this memory of his peaceful days passed in the capital, before the ambition of the Turkic general An Lu-shan had driven his master into exile in far Ssŭch'uan. The poet himself is speaking in the character of a lonely old man, wandering slowly down the winding banks of the river Kio.

' "Alas!" he murmured, "they are closed, the thousand palace doors, mirrored in clear cool waters. The young willows and the rushes renewing with the year—for whom will they now grow green?"

'Once in the garden of the South waved the standard of the Emperor.

'All that nature yields was there, vying with the rarest hues.

'There lived she whom the love of the first of men had made first among women.

'She who rode in the imperial chariot, in the excursions on sunny days.

'Before the chariot flashed the bright escort of maidens armed with bow and arrow,

'Mounted upon white steeds which pawed the ground, champing their golden bits.

'Gaily they raised their heads, launching their arrows into the clouds,

'And, laughing, uttered joyous cries when a bird fell victim to their skill.'

In the city of Ch'ang-an, with its triple rows of glittering walls with their tall towers uprising at intervals, its seven royal palaces all girdled with gardens, its wonderful Yen tower nine stories high, encased in marble, the drum towers and bell towers, the canals and lakes with their floating theatres, dwelt Ming Huang and T'ai-Chên. Within the royal park on the borders of the lake stood a little pavilion round whose balcony crept jasmine and magnolia branches scenting the air. Just underneath flamed a tangle of peonies in bloom, leaning down to the calm blue waters. Here in the evening the favourite reclined, watching the peonies vie with the sunset beyond. Here the Emperor sent his minister for Li Po, and here the great lyrist set her mortal beauty to glow from the scented, flower-haunted balustrade immortally through the twilights yet to come.

> What matter if the snow
> Blot out the garden? She shall still recline
> Upon the scented balustrade and glow
> With spring that thrills her warm blood into wine.

Once, and once alone, the artist in Ming Huang was merged in the Emperor. In that supreme crisis of the empire and a human soul, when the mutinous soldiers were thronging about the royal tent and clamouring for the blood of the favourite, it was the Emperor who sent her forth—

> lily pale,
> Between tall avenues of spears, to die.

Policy, the bane of artists demanded it, and so, for the sake of a thousand issues and a common front to the common foe, he placed the love of his life upon the altar of his patriotism, and went, a broken-hearted

23

man, into the long exile. From that moment the Emperor died. History ceases to take interest in the crownless wanderer. His return to the place of tragedy, and on to the capital where the deserted palace awaits him with its memories, his endless seeking for the soul of his beloved, her discovery by the priest of Tao in that island of P'eng Lai where—

> gaily coloured towers
> Rise up like rainbow clouds, and many gentle
> And beautiful Immortals pass their days in peace,

her message to her lover with its splendid triumphant note of faith foretelling their reunion at the last —in fine, the story of their love with the grave between them—is due to the genius of Po Chü-i. And to all poets coming after, these two lovers have been types of romantic and mystic love between man and woman. Through them the symbols of the mandarin duck and drake, the one-winged birds, the tree whose boughs are interwoven, are revealed. They are the earthly counterparts of the heavenly lovers, the Cowherd and the Spinning-maid in the constellations of Lyra and Aquila. To them Chinese poetry owes some of its finest inspirations, and at least two of its greatest singers, Tu Fu and Li Po.

CHINESE VERSE FORM

In passing it is necessary to refer to the structure of Chinese verse, which, difficult as it is to grasp and differing in particulars from our European ideas of technique, has considerable interest for the student of verse form and construction.

The favourite metres of the T'ang poets were in lines of five or seven syllables. There is no fixed rule as regards the length of a poem, but, generally speaking, they were composed of four, eight, twelve, or sixteen lines. Only the even lines rhyme, except in the four-line or stop-short poem, when the first line often rhymes with the second and fourth, curiously recalling the Rubaiyat form of the Persian poets. There is also a break or cæsura which in five-syllable verses falls after the second syllable and in seven-syllable verses after the fourth. The Chinese also make use of two kinds of tone in their poetry, the Ping or even, and the Tsze or oblique.

The even tone has two variations differing from each other only in pitch; the oblique tone has three variations, known as 'Rising, Sinking, and Entering'. In a seven-syllable verse the odd syllables can have any tone; as regards the even syllables, when the second syllable is even, then the fourth is oblique, and the sixth even. Furthermore, lines two and three, four and five, six and seven, have the same tones on the even syllables. The origin of the Chinese tone is not a poetical one, but is undoubtedly due to the necessity of having some distinguishing method of accentuation in a language which only contains about four hundred different sounds.

Introduction

THE INFLUENCE OF RELIGION ON CHINESE POETRY

To Confucius, as has been already stated, is due that groundwork of Chinese poetry—the Odes. But the master gave his fellow countrymen an ethical system based upon sound common sense, and a deep knowledge of their customs and characteristics. There is little in the Confucian classics to inspire a poet, and we must turn to Buddhism and the mystical philosophy of Lao Tzŭ for any source of spiritual inspiration from which the poets have drawn. Buddhism and Taoism are sisters. Their parents are self-observance and the Law. Both are quietists, yet in this respect they differ, that the former is the grey quietist, the latter the pearl. The neutral tint is better adapted to the sister in whose eyes all things are Maya—illusion. The shimmer of pearl belongs of right to her whose soul reflects the colour and quiet radiance of a thousand dreams. Compassion urged the one, the love of harmony led the other. How near they were akin! how far apart they have wandered! Yet there has always been this essential difference between them, that while the Buddhist regards the senses as windows looking out upon unreality and mirage, to the Taoist they are doors through which the freed soul rushes to mingle with the colours and tones and contours of the universe. Both Buddha and Lao Tzŭ are poets, one listening to the rhythm of infinite sorrow, one to the rhythm of infinite joy. Neither knows anything of reward at the hands of men or angels. The teaching of the Semitic religions, 'Do good to others that you may benefit at their hands', does not occur in their pages, nor any hints of sensuous delights hereafter. In all the great Buddhist poems, of which the Shu Hsing Tsan Ching is the best example, there is the same deep sadness, the haunting sorrow of doom. To look on beautiful things is only to feel more poignantly the passing of bright days, and the time when the petals must leave the rose. The form of desire hides within it the seeds of decay. In this epic of which I have spoken, Buddha sees the lovely and virtuous Lady Aruna coming to greet him, says to his disciples:

'This woman is indeed exceedingly beautiful, able to fascinate the minds of the religious; so then keep your recollections straight! Let wisdom keep your mind in subjection! Better fall into the fierce tiger's mouth, or under the sharp knife of the executioner, than to dwell with a woman. . . . A woman is anxious to exhibit her form and shape, whether walking, standing, sitting, or even sleeping; even when represented as a picture, she desires most of all to set off the blandishments of her beauty, and thus rob men of their steadfast heart! How then ought you to guard yourselves? By regarding her tears and her smiles as enemies, her stooping form, her hanging arms, and all her disentangled hair as toils designed to entrap man's heart. Then how much more should you suspect her studied, amorous beauty! when she displays her dainty outline, her richly ornamented form, and chatters gaily with the foolish man! Ah, then! what perturbation and what evil thoughts, not seeing underneath the sorrows of impermanence, the impurity, the unreality! Considering these as the reality, all desires die out.' [1]

How different is this meeting of beauty and Buddhism from the meeting of Ssü-K'ung T'u, the great Taoist poet, with an unknown girl!

> Gathering the water-plants
> From the wild luxuriance of spring,
> Away in the depth of a wild valley
> Anon, I see a lovely girl.
> With green leaves the peach-trees are loaded,
> The breeze blows gently along the stream,
> Willows shade the winding path,
> Darting orioles collect in groups.
> Eagerly I press forward
> As the reality grows upon me. . . .
> 'Tis the eternal theme,
> Which, though old, is ever new. [2]

Here is reality emerging from the unreal, spring renewing, love and beauty triumphant over death and decay. The girl is the central type and symbol. From her laughing eyes a thousand dead women look out once more on spring, through her poets find their inspiration. Beauty is the key that unlocks the secrets of the frozen world, and brings the dead to life again.

The Symbol of Decay!

The Symbol of Immortality!

It is perhaps both. There are times when the grave

[1] *Sacred Books of the East*, vol. xix, pp. 253-4.
[2] *History of Chinese Literature*, by Professor Herbert Giles, p. 180.

words of the Dhammapada fall like shadows along the path: 'What is life but the flower or the fruit which falls when ripe, yet ever fears the untimely frost? Once born, there is naught but sorrow; for who is there can escape death? From the first moment of life, the result of passionate love and desire, there is nought but the bodily form transitional as the lightning flash.' Yet apart from all transitory passions and the ephemeral results of mortal love, the song of the Taoist lover soars unstained, untrammelled. Man attains not by himself, nor woman by herself, but, like the one-winged birds of the Chinese legend, they must rise together. To be a great lover is to be a great mystic, since in the highest conception of mortal beauty that the mind can form there lies always the unattainable, the unpossessed, suggesting the world of beauty and finality beyond our mortal reach. It is in this power of suggestion that the Chinese poets excel. Asked to differentiate between European and Chinese poetry, some critics would perhaps insist upon their particular colour sense, instancing the curious fact that where we see blue to them it often appears green, and vice versa, or the tone theories that make their poems so difficult to understand; in fact, a learned treatise would be written on these lines, to prove that the Chinese poets were not human beings as we understand humanity at all. It is, however, not by this method that we can begin to trace the difference between the poets of East and West, but in the two aspects of life which no amount of comparison can reconcile.

Introduction

To the Chinese such commonplace things as marriage, friendship, and home have an infinitely deeper meaning than can be attached to them by civilization which practically lives abroad, in the hotels and restaurants and open houses of others, where there is no sanctity of the life within, no shrine set apart for the hidden family reunion, and the cult of the ancestral spirit. To the Western world, life, save for the conventional hour or so set aside on the seventh day, is a thing profane. In the far East the head of every family is a high-priest in the calling of daily life. It is for this reason that a quietism is to be found in Chinese poetry ill appealing to the unrest of our day, and as dissimilar to our ideals of existence as the life of the planets is to that of the dark bodies whirling aimlessly through space.

The Odes of Confucius

1765–585 B.C.

Collected by Confucius about 500 B.C.

❄ ❄

SADNESS

The sun is ever full and bright,
The pale moon waneth night by night.
     Why should this be?

My heart that once was full of light
Is but a dying moon to-night.

But when I dream of thee apart,
I would the dawn might lift my heart,
     O sun, to thee.

❄ ❄

TRYSTING TIME

I

A pretty girl at time o' gloaming
Hath whispered me to go and meet her
     Without the city gate.

I love her, but she tarries coming.
Shall I return, or stay and greet her?
      I burn, and wait.

II

Truly she charmeth all beholders,
'Tis she hath given me this jewel,
    The jade of my delight;
But this red jewel-jade that smoulders,
To my desire doth add more fuel,
      New charms to-night.

III

She has gathered with her lily fingers
  A lily fair and rare to see.
Oh! sweeter still the fragrance lingers
  From the warm hand that gave it me.

❄ ❄

THE SOLDIER

I climbed the barren mountain,
  And my gaze swept far and wide
For the red-lit eaves of my father's home,
  And I fancied that he sighed:
    My son has gone for a soldier,
      For a soldier night and day;
    But my son is wise, and may yet return,
      When the drums have died away.

I climbed the grass-clad mountain,
  And my gaze swept far and wide
For the rosy lights of a little room,
    Where I thought my mother sighed:
      My boy has gone for a soldier,
        He sleeps not day and night;
      But my boy is wise, and may yet return,
        Though the dead lie far from sight.

I climbed the topmost summit,
  And my gaze swept far and wide
For the garden roof where my brother stood,
    And I fancied that he sighed:
      My brother serves as a soldier
        With his comrades night and day;
      But my brother is wise, and may yet return,
        Though the dead lie far away.

Ch'ü Yüan

FOURTH CENTURY, B.C.

A loyal minister to the feudal Prince of Ch'ü, towards the close of the Chou dynasty. His master having, through disregard of his counsel, been captured by the Ch'in State, Ch'ü Yüan sank into disfavour with his sons, and retired to the hills, where he wrote his famous *Li Sao*, of which the following is one of the songs. He eventually drowned himself in the river Mi-Lo, and in spite of the search made for his body, it was never found. The Dragon-boat Festival, held on the fifth day of the fifth moon, was founded in his honour.

❀ ❀

THE LAND OF EXILE

Methinks there's a genius
Roams in the mountains,
Girdled with ivy
And robed in wisteria,
Lips ever smiling,
Of noble demeanour,
Driving the yellow pard,
Tiger-attended,
Couched in a chariot
With banners of cassia,

Cloaked with the orchid,
And crowned with azaleas;
Culling the perfume
Of sweet flowers, he leaves
In the heart a dream-blossom,
Memory haunting.
But dark is the forest
Where now is my dwelling,
Never the light of day
Reaches its shadow.
Thither a perilous
Pathway meanders.
Lonely I stand
On the lonelier hill-top,
Cloudland beneath me
And cloudland around me.
Softly the wind bloweth,
Softly the rain falls,
Joy like a mist blots
The thoughts of my home out;
There none would honour me,
Fallen from honours.
I gather the larkspur
Over the hillside,
Blown mid the chaos
Of boulder and bellbine;
Hating the tyrant
Who made me an outcast,
Who of his leisure
Now spares me no moment:

Ch'ü Yüan

Drinking the mountain spring,
Shading at noon-day
Under the cypress
My limbs from the sun glare.
What though he summon me
Back to his palace,
I cannot fall
To the level of princes.
Now rolls the thunder deep,
Down the cloud valley,
And the gibbons around me
Howl in the long night.
The gale through the moaning trees
Fitfully rushes.
Lonely and sleepless
I think of my thankless
Master, and vainly would
Cradle my sorrow.

Wang Seng-ju

SIXTH CENTURY, A.D.

❀ ❀

TEARS

High o'er the hill the moon barque steers.
    The lantern lights depart.
Dead springs are stirring in my heart,
      And there are tears. . . .
But that which makes my grief more deep
Is that you know not when I weep.

Ch'ên Tzǔ-ang

A.D. 656–698

Famous for writing that kind of impromptu descriptive verse which the Chinese call 'Ying'. In temperament he was less Chinese than most of his contemporaries. His passionate disposition finally brought him into trouble with the magistrate of his district, who had him cast into prison, where he died at the age of forty-two.

Whatever his outward demeanour may have been, his poetry gives us no indication of it, being full of delicate mysticism, almost impossible to reproduce in the English language. For this reason I have chosen one of his simpler poems as a specimen.

❁ ❁

THE LAST REVEL

From silver lamps a thin blue smoke is streaming,
And golden vases 'mid the feast are gleaming;
    Now sound the lutes in unison,
    Within the gates our lives are one.
    We'll think not of the parting ways
    As long as dawn delays.

When in tall trees the dying moonbeams quiver:
When floods of fire efface the Silver River,

Then comes the hour when I must seek
Lo-Yang beyond the furthest peak.
But the warm twilight round us twain
    Will never rise again.

Sung Chih-Wên

DIED A.D. 710

The son of a distinguished general, he began his career as
attaché to the military advisers of the Emperor. These advisers
were always drawn from the literary class, and their duties
appear to have been chiefly administrative and diplomatic. Of
his life, the less said the better. He became involved in a palace
intrigue, and only saved himself by betraying his accomplices.
In the end he was banished, and finally put to death by the
Emperor's order. It is necessary, however, to dissociate the
man from his poetry, and Sung Chih-Wên's poetry often touches
a high level of inspiration.

✤❦ ❦✤

THE COURT OF DREAMS

Rain from the mountains of Ki-Sho
Fled swiftly with a tearing breeze;
The sun came radiant down the west,
And greener blushed the valley trees.

I entered through the convent gate:
The abbot bade me welcome there,
And in the court of silent dreams
I lost the thread of worldly care.

That holy man and I were one,
Beyond the bounds that words can trace:
The very flowers were still as we.
I heard the lark that hung in space,
And Truth Eternal flashed on me.

Kao-Shih

CIRCA A.D. 700

One of the most fascinating of all the T'ang poets. His life was one long series of romantic adventure. At first, a poor youth battling with adversity; then the lover of an actress, whom he followed through the provinces, play-writing for the strolling troupe to which she was attached; the next, secretary to a high personage engaged in a mission to Thibet; then soldier, and finally poet of renown, acquiring with his latter years the fortune and honours denied him in his youth.

The chief characteristics of his poetry are intense concentration, a vivid power of impressionism, and a strong leaning in the direction of the occult. Indeed, one of his best-known poems, 'The Return to the Mountains', makes mention of the projection of the astral body through space during sleep. Many of his poems leave us with a strange sense of horror which is suggested rather than revealed. It is always some combination of effects which produces this result, and never a concrete form.

❖ ❖

IMPRESSIONS OF A TRAVELLER

In a silent, desolate spot,
In the night stone-frozen and clear,
The wanderer's hand on the sail
Is gripped by the fingers of fear.

He looketh afar o'er the waves,
Wind-ruffled and deep and green;
And the mantle of Autumn lies
Over wood and hill and ravine.

'Tis Autumn!—time of decay,
And the dead leaves' 'wildering flight;
And the mantle of Autumn lies
On the wanderer's soul to-night!

❦ ❧

DESOLATION

I

There was a King of Liang[1]—a king of wondrous
    might—
Who kept an open palace, where music charmed the
    night—

II

Since he was Lord of Liang a thousand years have
    flown,
And of the towers he builded yon ruin stands alone.

III

There reigns a heavy silence; gaunt weeds through
    windows pry,
And down the streets of Liang old echoes, wailing, die.

[1] Strictly speaking, the pronunciation of all words such as Liang,
Kiang, etc., is nearer one syllable than two. For purposes of euphony
however, without which the lines would be harsh and unpoetical, I
have invariably made two syllables of them.

Mêng Hao-jan

A.D. 689–740

One of the few literary men of the day whose later life was
devoted entirely to literature. He was the inseparable friend of
the famous Buddhist poet and doctor, Wang Wei. He spent the
first forty years of his life in acquiring knowledge, but having
failed to obtain his doctor's degree, he returned to the quiet
hills of his native province and dedicated his remaining years to
composition. Most of his poems, other than certain political
satire, which drew on him the Emperor's wrath, are full of
subtle sadness and fragrant regret, reminding one of pot-pourri
in some deep blue porcelain bowl.

❀ ❀

THE LOST ONE

The red gleam o'er the mountains
   Goes wavering from sight,
And the quiet moon enhances
   The loveliness of night.

I open wide my casement
   To breathe the rain-cooled air.
And mingle with the moonlight
   The dark waves of my hair.

The night wind tells me secrets
  Of lotus lilies blue;
And hour by hour the willows
  Shake down the chiming dew.

I fain would take the zither,
  By some stray fancy led;
But there are none to hear me,
  And who can charm the dead?

So all my day-dreams follow
  The bird that leaves the nest;
And in the night I gather
  The lost one to my breast.

❀ ❀

A FRIEND EXPECTED

Over the chain of giant peaks
  The great red sun goes down,
And in the stealthy floods of night
  The distant valleys drown.

Yon moon that cleaves the gloomy pines
  Has freshness in her train;
Low wind, faint stream, and waterfall
  Haunt me with their refrain.

The tired woodman seeks his cot
  That twinkles up the hill;

Mêng Hao-jan

And sleep has touched the wanderers
    That sang the twilight still.

To-night—ah! beauty of to-night
    I need my friend to praise,
So take the lute to lure him on
    Through the fragrant, dew-lit ways.

Ch'ang Ch'ien

CIRCA A.D. 720

One of the great philosopher-poets of the Taoist school. His life was spent far from the court and away from the sounds of civil warfare, in the endeavour to set himself in harmony with the universe—to become, in fact, like an Æolian harp through which all the chords of nature might sweep at will. How far he attained the end desired may be seen in his work, which is penetrated by a sense of profound beauty, recalling the quiet twilight upon the mountain-side, which he so well describes.

A NIGHT ON THE MOUNTAIN

I sat upon the mountain-side and watched
A tiny barque that skimmed across the lake,
Drifting, like human destiny upon
A world of hidden peril; then she sailed
From out my ken, and mingled with the blue
Of skies unfathomed, while the great round sun
Weakened towards the waves.
                The whole expanse
Suddenly in the half-light of the dusk
Glimmered and waned. The last rays of the sun
Lit but the tops of trees and mountain-peaks

Ch'ang Ch'ien

With tarnished glory; and the water's sheen,
Once blue and bright, grew lustreless, and soon
A welter of red clouds alone betrayed
The passing of the sun. The scattered isles
Uprose, black-looming o'er the tranquil deeps,
Where the reflected heavens wanly showed
A lingering gleam. Already wood and hill
Sank in obscurity. The river marge
Seemed but a broken line to failing sight.

.   .   .   .   .

Night is at hand; the night winds fret afar,
The North winds moan. The waterfowl are gone
To cover o'er the sand-dunes; dawn alone
Shall call them from the sedges. Some bright star

Mirrors her charms upon the silver shoal;
And I have ta'en the lute, my only friend:
The vibrant chords beneath my fingers blend;
They sob awhile, then as they slip control

Immortal memories awake, and the dead years
Through deathless voices answer to my strings,
Till from the brink of Time's untarnished springs
The melting night recalls me with her tears.

Ts'ên-Ts'an

CIRCA A.D. 750

Of his life we know little, save that he was the intimate friend
of the great poet Tu Fu, and came of a noble family. He was,
moreover, Censor under the Emperor Su Tsung (A.D. 756–762),
and rose to be Governor of Chia-chou. What remains of his
verse mostly takes the form of quatrains, yet for originality of
thought, wealth of imagery and style, they have seldom been
excelled. He was a master of metre, and contributed certain
modifications to the laws of Chinese prosody which exist to the
present day.

❀❀ ❀❀

A DREAM OF SPRING

Last night within my chamber's gloom some vague
    light breath of Spring
Came wandering and whispering, and bade my soul
    take wing.

A hundred moonlit miles away the Chiang crept to
    sea;
O keeper of my heart, I came by Chiang's ford to thee.
It lingered but a moment's space, that dream of Spring
    and died;

Ts'ên-Ts'an

Yet as my head the pillows pressed, my soul had found
thy side.

Oh! Chiang Nan's a hundred miles, yet in a moment's
space
I've flown away to Chiang Nan and touched a dreaming face.

Tu Fu

A.D. 712–770

Tu Fu, whom his countrymen called the God of Verse, was born in the province of Hu-Kuang, and this was his portrait from contemporaries:

He was tall and slightly built, yet robust with finely chiselled features; his manners were exquisite, and his appearance distinguished. He came of a literary family, and, as he says of himself, from his seventh to his fortieth year study and letters occupied all his available time. At the age of twenty-seven he came to the capital with his fame in front of him, and there Li Po the poet and Ts'ên Ts'an became his friends, and Ming Huang his patron. He obtained a post at Court somewhat similar to that of Master of Ceremonies in our own Court. Yet the poet had few sympathies outside the artistic life. He was so unwordly and so little of a courtier that when the new Emperor Su Tsung returned in triumph to the capital and appointed him Imperial Censor, he fulfilled his new duties by telling his majesty the whole unpalatable truth in a manner strangely free from ornamental apology, and was promptly rewarded with the exile of a provincial governorship. But Tu Fu was no man of affairs, and knew it. On the day of his public installation he took off his insignia of office before the astonished notables, and, laying them one by one on the table, made them a profound reverence, and quietly withdrew.

Like his friend Li Po, he became a homeless wanderer, but, unlike him, he concealed his brilliant name, obtaining food and patronage for his delightful nameless self alone, and not for his reputation's sake. Finally, he was discovered by the military governor of the province of Ssŭch'uan, who applied on his behalf for the post of Restorer of Ancient Monuments in the district, the one congenial appointment of his life. For six years he kept his post; then trouble in the shape of rebel hordes burst once more upon the province, and again he became an exile. The last act of this eventful life took place in his native district: some local mandarin gave a great banquet in honour of the distinguished poet, whom he had rescued, half drowned and famishing, from the ruined shrine by the shore where the waters had cast him up. The wine-cup brimmed again and again, food was piled up in front of the honoured guest, and the attendant who waited was Death. The end was swift, sudden, and pitiful. The guest died from the banquet of his rescuer.

Of all poets Tu Fu is the first in craftsmanship. It is interesting to add that he was a painter as well, and the friend of painters, notably the soldier-artist, Kiang-Tu, to whom he dedicates a poem. Possibly it is to this faculty that he owes his superb technique. He seeks after simplicity and its effects as a diver seeks for sunken gold. In his poem called 'The Little Rain', which I have (perhaps somewhat rashly) attempted, there is all the graciousness of fine rain falling upon sullen furrows, which charms the world into spring. 'The Recruiting Sergeant' has the touch of grim desolation, which belongs inevitably to a country plundered of its men and swept with the ruinous winds of rebellion.

Li Po give us Watteau-like pictures of life in Ch'ang-an before the flight of the Emperor. The younger poet paints, with the brush of Verestchagin, the realism and horrors of civil war. In most of Tu Fu's work there is an underlying sadness which appears continually, sometimes in the vein that runs throughout the poem, sometimes at the conclusion, and often at the summing up of all things. Other poets have it, some more, some less, with the exception of those who belong to the purely Taoist school. The reason is that the Chinese poet is haunted. He is haunted by the vast shadow of a past without historians—a past that is legendary, unmapped and unbounded, and yields, therefore, Golcondas and golden lands innumerable to its bold adventurers. He is haunted from out the crumbled palaces of vanished kings, where 'in the form of blue flames one sees spirits moving through each dark recess'. He is haunted by the traditional voices of the old masters of his craft, and lastly, more than all, by the dead women and men of his race, the ancestors that count in the making of his composite soul and have their silent say in every action, thought, and impulse of his life.

❦ ❦

THE LITTLE RAIN

Oh! she is good, the little rain! and well she knows
    our need
Who cometh in the time of spring to aid the sun-
    drawn seed;
She wanders with a friendly wind through silent nights
    unseen,
The furrows feel her happy tears, and lo! the land is
    green.

Last night cloud-shadows gloomed the path that winds
    to my abode,
And the torches of the river-boats like angry meteors
    glowed.
To-day fresh colours break the soil, and butterflies
    take wing
Down broidered lawns all bright with pearls in the
    garden of the King.

❦ ❦

A NIGHT OF SONG

The wind scarce flutters through the leaves,
The young moon hath already gone,

And kind and cool the dews descend:
The lute-strings wake for night alone.

In shadow lapse the twinkling streams,
The lilied marge their waves caress;
And the sheer constellations sway
O'er soundless gulfs of nothingness.

What cadence charms the poet's ear!
What fire-fly fancies round him swarm!
He dreads the lantern lights may fail
Long ere his thoughts have taken form.

Now gallants tap their two-edged swords,
And pride and passion swell amain;
Like red stars flashing through the night
The circling wine-cups brim again.

There steals the old sad air of Ou—
Each calls his latest song to mind;
Then white sails taper down the stream,
While lingering thoughts still look behind.

❀ ❀

THE RECRUITING SERGEANT

At sunset in the village of Che-Kao[1]
I sought for shelter; on my heels there trod

[1] All words ending in *ao* are pronounced *ow*, as in English *vow*, *allow*, etc.

The Recruiting Sergeant

A grim recruiting sergeant, of the kind
That seize their prey by night. A poor old man
Saw—scaled the wall, and vanished. Through the gate
An old bent woman hobbled, and she marched
A pace before him. Loudly in his wrath
The grim recruiter stormed; and bitterly
She answered: 'Listen to the voice of her
Who drags before you. Once I had three sons—
Three in the Emperor's camp. A letter came
From one, and—there was one; the others fell
In the same battle—he alone was left,
Scarce able from the iron grasp of Death
To tear his miserable life.
                                        Alas
My two dead boys! for ever and for aye
Death holds them. In our wretched hut remains
The last of all the men—a little child,
Still at his mother's breast. She cannot flee.
Since her few tatters scarce suffice to clothe
Her shrunken limbs.
                                My years are nearly done,
My strength is well-nigh spent; yet I will go
Readily to the camping-ground. Perchance
I may be useful for some humble task,
To cook the rice or stir the morning meal.'

.   .   .   .   .   .

Night slipped away. The clamour and the cries
Died down; but there was weeping and the sound
Of stifled moans around me.

> At the break
Of dawn I hurried on my road, and left
None but an old and broken man behind.

❀ ❀

CHANTS OF AUTUMN

Shorn by the frost with crystal blade,
The dry leaves, scattered, fall at last;
Among the valleys of Wu Chan
Cold winds of death go wailing past.
Tumultuous waves of the great river rise
And seem to storm the skies,
While snow-bright peak and prairie mist combine,
And greyness softens the harsh mountain line.

Chrysanthemums unfurl to-day,
To-morrow the last flowers are blown.
I am the barque that chains delay:
My homeward thoughts must sail alone.
From house to house warm winter robes are spread,
And through the pine-woods red
Floats up the sound of the washerman's bat who plies
His hurried task ere the brief noon wanes and dies.

Li Po

A.D. 702–762

The most famous name in Chinese literature. Born in the province of Ssŭch'uan, Li Po obtained his doctor's degree at the age of twenty, and was already known as a brilliant, inspired poet before Ming Huang became his patron in the capital. A suite of rooms overlooking the beautiful gardens of T'eng-hsiang T'ing, where the Emperor retired after the routine of the day, was assigned to him. Here the poet improvised, whilst Ming Huang himself wrote down the verses that he afterwards set to music, and accompanied while the poet sang. But Li Po, with all his enthusiasm for his patron and the delights of the garden-life, was little of a courtier. When Ming Huang bade the masterful eunuch Kao Li-shih unlace the poet's boots, he gave him a relentless enemy whose malice pursued him, until at length he was glad to beg leave to retire from the court, where he was never at ease and to which he never returned. Trouba-dour-like, he wandered through the provinces, the guest of mandarin and local governor, the star of the drinking-taverns, the delight and embarrassment of all his hosts. At length a friend of former days, to whom he had attached himself, un-happily involved him in the famous rebellion of An Lu-shan. The poet was seized and thrown into prison. Yet prison doors were ill warders of his fame, and letters of recall followed closely upon pardon; but death overtook the exile before he could reach the capital, and at the age of sixty his wanderings came to an end.

Li Po was a poet with a sword by his side. He would have ruffled bravely with our Elizabethans, and for a Chinese is strangely warlike in sentiment. How he loves the bravo of Chao with his sabre from the Chinese Sheffield of Wu, 'with the surface smooth as ice and dazzling as snow, with his saddle broidered with silver upon his white steed; who when he passes, swift as the wind, may be said to resemble a shooting star!' He compares the frontiersman, who has never so much as opened a book in all his life, yet knows how to follow in the chase, and is skilful, strong, and hardy, with the men of his own profession. 'From these intrepid wanderers how different our literary men who grow grey over their books behind a curtained window.'

It is harder to write of Li Po than of any other Chinese poet. Po Chu-i has his own distinctive feeling for romance, Tu Fu his minute literary craftsmanship, Ssŭ-K'ung T'u the delicate aroma of suggestive mysticism; but Li Po is many-sided, and has perhaps more of the world-spirit than all of them. We can imagine this bold, careless, impulsive artist, with his moments of great exaltation and alternate depression, a kind of Chinese Paul Verlaine, with his sensitive mind of a child, always recording impressions as they come. T'ai Chên the beautiful and the grim frontiersman are alike faithfully portrayed. He lives for the moment, and the moment is often wine-flushed like the rosy glow of dawn, or grey and wan as the twilight of a hopeless day.

❧ ❧

TO THE CITY OF NAN-KING

Thou that hast seen six kingdoms pass away,
Accept my song and these three cups I drain!
There may be fairer gardens light the plain;
Thine are the dim blue hills more fair than they.

Here Kings of Wu were crowned and overthrown,
Where peaceful grass along the ruin wins;
Here—was it yesterday?—the royal Tsins
Called down the dreams of sunset into stone.

One end awaits for all that mortal be;
Pride and despair shall find a common grave:
The Yang-tse-kiang renders wave and wave
To mingle with the abysms of the sea.

❧ ❧

MEMORIES WITH THE DUSK RETURN

The yellow dusk winds round the city wall:
      The crows are drawn to nest,
      Silently down the west
They hasten home, and from the branches call.
A woman sits and weaves with fingers deft
    Her story of the flower-lit stream,
    Threading the jasper gauze in dream,
Till like faint smoke it dies; and she, bereft,
    Recalls the parting words that died
Under the casement some far eventide,
    And stays the disappointed loom,
    While from the little lonely room
    Into the lonely night she peers,
And, like the rain, unheeded fall her tears.

❧ ❧

AN EMPEROR'S LOVE

In all the clouds he sees her light robes trail,
And roses seem beholden to her face;
O'er scented balustrade the scented gale
Blows warm from Spring, and dew-drops form apace.

Li Po

Her outline on the mountain he can trace,
Now leans she from the tower in moonlight pale.

A flower-girt branch grows sweeter from the dew.
The spirit of snow and rain unheeded calls.
Who wakes to memory in these palace walls?
Fei-yen![1]—but in the robes an Empress knew.

The most renowned of blossoms, most divine
Of those whose conquering glances overthrow
Cities and kingdoms, for his sake combine
And win the ready smiles that ever flow
From royal lips. What matter if the snow
Blot out the garden? She shall still recline
Upon the scented balustrade and glow
With spring that thrills her warm blood into wine.

❧ ❧

ON THE BANKS OF JO-EH

They gather lilies down the stream,
A net of willows drooping low
Hides boat from boat; and to and fro
Sweet whispered confidences seem
    'Mid laughing trills to flow.

In the green deeps a shaft of gold
Limns their elaborate attire;

[1] A delicate compliment to the beautiful T'ai-Chên, of which the meaning is that, as the Emperor Yang-ti of the Sui dynasty elevated his mistress Fei-yen to share with him the throne, so shall T'ai-Chên become the Empress of Ming Huang.

Thoughts in a Tranquil Night

Through silken sleeves the winds aspire,
Embalmed, to stray, and, growing bold,
    Swell them to their desire.

But who are these, the cavaliers
That gleam along the river-side?
By three, by five they prance with pride
Beyond the willow-line that sheers
    Over the trellised tide.

A charger neighs; one turns to start,
Crushing the kingcups as he flies,
And one pale maiden vainly tries
To hush the tumult in her heart
And veil the secret of her eyes.

❦ ❦

THOUGHTS IN A TRANQUIL NIGHT

Athwart the bed
I watch the moonbeams cast a trail
So bright, so cold, so frail.
That for a space it gleams
Like hoar-frost on the margin of my dreams.
I raise my head,—
The splendid moon I see:
Then droop my head,
And sink to dreams of thee—
My Fatherland, of thee!

61

Li Po

The universe is but a tenement
Of all things visible. Darkness and day
The passing guests of Time. Life slips away,
A dream of little joy and mean content.

Ah! wise the old philosophers who sought
To lengthen their long sunsets among flowers,
By stealing the young night's unsullied hours
And the dim moments with sweet burdens fraught.

And now Spring beckons me with verdant hand,
And Nature's wealth of eloquence doth win
Forth to the fragrant-bowered nectarine,
Where my dear friends abide, a careless band.

There meet my gentle, matchless brothers, there
I come, the obscure poet, all unfit
To wear the radiant jewellery of wit,
And in their golden presence cloud the air.

And while the thrill of meeting lingers, soon
As the first courtly words, the feast is spread,
While, couched on flowers 'mid wine-cups flashing
    red,
We drink deep draughts unto The Lady Moon.

Then as without the touch of verse divine
There is no outlet for the pent-up soul,

'Twas ruled that he who quaffed no fancy's bowl
Should drain the 'Golden Valley' [1] cups of wine.

❀❀

UNDER THE MOON

Under the crescent moon's faint glow
The washerman's bat resounds afar,
And the autumn breeze sighs tenderly.
But my heart has gone to the Tartar war,
To bleak Kansuh and the steppes of snow,
Calling my husband back to me.

❀❀

DRIFTING

We cannot keep the gold of yesterday;
To-day's dun clouds we cannot roll away.
Now the long, wailing flight of geese brings autumn
in its train,
So to the view-tower cup in hand to fill and drink
again,

And dream of the great singers of the past,
Their fadeless lines of fire and beauty cast.
I too have felt the wild-bird thrill of song behind the
bars,

[1] i.e. drink three cups of wine, the 'Golden Valley' being the name of a garden, the owner of which enforced this penalty among his boon companions (*Gems of Chinese Literature*, p. 113).

Li Po

But these have brushed the world aside and walked
 amid the stars.

> In vain we cleave the torrent's thread with steel,
> In vain we drink to drown the grief we feel;

When man's desire with fate doth war this, this avails
 alone—
To hoist the sail and let the gale and the waters bear us
 on.

Wang Ch'ang-ling

CIRCA A.D. 750

This poet came from the district of Chiang-ning to the capital, where he obtained his doctor's degree and distinguished himself as a man of letters. For some time he filled a minor post, but was eventually disgraced and exiled to the province of Hunan. When the rebellion of An Lu-shan broke out, he returned to his native place, where he was cruelly murdered by the censor Lu Ch'in-hsiao. (See Hervey Saint-Denys, *Poésies des Thang*, p. 224; Giles, *Biog. Dict.*, p. 8087.)

❖ ❖

THE SONG OF THE NENUPHARS

Leaves of the Nenuphars and silken skirts the same
    pale green,
On flower and laughing face alike the same rose-tints
    are seen;
Like some blurred tapestry they blend within the lake
    displayed:
You cannot part the leaves from silk, the lily from the
    maid.

      Only when sudden voices swell
      Do maidens of their presence tell.

Wang Ch'ang-ling

Here long ago the girls of Su, the darlings of the King,
Dabbled their shining skirts with dew from the
   gracious blooms of Spring.
When to the lake's sun-dimpled marge the bright
   procession wends,
The languid lilies raise their heads as though to greet
   their friends;
   When down the river-banks they roam,
   The white moon-lady leads them home.

❦ ❦

TEARS IN THE SPRING

Clad in blue silk and bright embroidery
At the first call of Spring the fair young bride,
On whom as yet Sorrow has laid no scar,
Climbs the Kingfisher's Tower. Suddenly
She sees the bloom of willows far and wide,
And grieves for him she lent to fame and war.

Chang Chih-ho

CIRCA A.D. 750

A Taoist philosopher who lived in the time of the Emperor Su Tsung, and held office under him. For some offence he was exiled, and the royal pardon found him far too occupied to dream of return.

Like so many of the same philosophy, he became a lonely wanderer, calling himself the 'Old Fisherman of the Mists and Waters'. Professor Giles (*Chinese Literature*, p. 191) adds the curious statement that 'he spent his time in angling, but used no bait, his object not being to catch fish'.

❀ ❀

A WORLD APART

The Lady Moon is my lover,
  My friends are the oceans four,
The heavens have roofed me over,
  And the dawn is my golden door.
I would liefer follow the condor
  Or the seagull, soaring from ken,
Than bury my godhead yonder
  In the dust of the whirl of men.

Chang Jo-hu

CIRCA A.D. 800

❀ ❀

When heaven reveals her primal stainless blue,
Alone within the firmament there burns
The tiny torch of dusk. What startled eyes
Uplifted from the restless stream first met
The full round glory of the moon! Yon orb
That pales upon the flood of broad Chiang,
When did she first through twilight mists unveil
Her wonders to the world?

                    Men come and go;
New generations hunger at the heels
Of those that yield possession. Still the moon
Fulfils her phases. While the tides of time
Eat out the rocks of empire, and the stars
Of human destiny adown the void
Go glittering to their doom, she changeless sweeps
Through all her times and destinies. Alas!
The little lives that swarmed beneath the moon,
I cannot count them. This alone I know—
That, wave on wave, the Chiang seeks the sea,
And not a wave returns.

One small white cloud
Threading the vasty vault of heaven recalls
My heart unto her loneliness. I sail
Between two banks, where heavy boughs enlace,
Whose verdurous luxuriance wakes once more
My many griefs. None know me as I am,
Steering to strange adventure. None may tell
If, steeped in the same moonlight, lies afar
Some dim pavilion where my lady dreams
Of me. Ah, happy moon! low lingering moon!
That with soft touch now brightens into jade
Lintel and door, and when she lifts the blind
Floats through the darkened chamber of her sleep;
While leagues away my love-winged messages
Go flocking home; and though they mingle not,
Our thoughts seek one another. In the lilt
Of winds I hear her whisper: 'Oh that I
Might melt into the moonbeams, and with them
Leap through the void, and shed myself with them
Upon my lover.' Slow the night creeps on.
Sleep harbours in the little room. She dreams—
Dreams of a fall o' flowers. Alas! young Spring
Lies on the threshold of maternity,
And still he comes not. Still the flowing stream
Sweeps on, but the swift torrents of green hours
Are licked into the brazen skies between
Their widening banks. The great deliberate moon
Now leans towards the last resort of night,
Gloom of the western waves. She dips her rim,
She sinks, she founders in the mist; and still

Chang Jo-hu

The stream flows on, and to the insatiate sea
Hurries her white-wave flocks innumerable
In never-ending tale. On such a night
How many tireless travellers may attain
The happy goal of their desire! So dreams
My lady till the moon goes down, and lo!
A rush of troubled waters floods her soul,
While black forebodings rise from deeps unknown
And the cold trail of fear creeps round her heart.

T'ung Han-ching

CIRCA A.D. 800

❧ ❧

THE CELESTIAL WEAVER

A thing of stone beside Lake Kouen-ming
Has for a thousand autumns borne the name
Of the Celestial Weaver. Like that star
She shines above the waters, wondering
At her pale loveliness. Unnumbered waves
Have broidered with green moss the marble folds
About her feet. Toiling eternally
They knock the stone, like tireless shuttles plied
Upon a sounding loom.
                              Her pearly locks
Resemble snow-coils on the mountain top;
Her eyebrows arch—the crescent moon. A smile
Lies in the opened lily of her face;
And, since she breathes not, being stone, the birds
Light on her shoulders, flutter without fear
At her still breast. Immovable she stands
Before the shining mirror of her charms
And, gazing on their beauty, lets the years
Slip into centuries past her. . . .

Po Chü-i

A.D. 772–846

Seventeen years old and already a doctor of letters, a great future was before him. The life of such a man would seem to be one sure progress from honour to honour. Yet it is to some petty exile, some temporary withdrawal of imperial favour, that we owe 'The Lute Girl', perhaps the most delicate piece of work that has survived the age of the golden T'angs. Certainly the music is the most haunting, suggestive of many-coloured moods, with an undertone of sadness, and that motive of sympathy between the artist-exiles of the universe which calls the song from the singer and tears from the heart of the man. So exile brought its consolations, the voice and presence of 'The Lute Girl', and the eight nameless poets who became with Po Chü-i the literary communists of Hsiang-shan. In China it has always been possible for the artist to live away from the capital. Provincial governor and high official send for him; all compete for the honour of his presence. Respect, which is the first word of Chinese wisdom according to Confucius, is paid to him. In provincial Europe his very presence would be unknown unless he beat his wife on the high-road or stole a neighbour's pig. But his Celestial Majesty hears of the simple life at Hsiang-shan and becomes jealous for his servant. The burden of ruling must once more be laid on not too willing shoulders. Po Chü-i is recalled and promoted from province to province, till eventually, five years before his death, he is made President of the Board of War. Two short poems here rendered—namely, 'Peaceful Old Age' and 'The Penalties of Rank'—give us a glimpse of the poet in his old age, conscious of decaying powers, glad to be quit of office, and waiting with sublime faith in his Taoist principles to be 'one with the pulsings of Eternity'.

Po Chü-i

Po Chü-i is almost nearer to the Western idea of a poet than any other Chinese writer. He was fortunate enough to be born when the great love-tragedy of Ming Huang and T'ai Chen was still fresh in the minds of men. He had the right perspective, being not too near and yet able to see clearly. He had, moreover, the feeling for romance which is so ill-defined in other poets of his country, though strongly evident in Chinese legend and story. He is an example of that higher patriotism rarely met with in Chinese official life which recognizes a duty to the Emperor as Father of the national family—a duty too often forgotten in the obligation to the clan and the desire to use power for personal advantage. Passionately devoted to literature, he might, like Li Po and Tu Fu, have set down the seals of office and lived for art alone by the mountain-side of his beloved Hsiang-shan. But no one knew better than Po Chü-i that from him that hath much, much shall be expected. The poet ennobled political life, the broader outlook of affairs enriched his poetry and humanized it.

And when some short holiday brought him across the frontier, and the sunlight, breaking out after a noon of rain over the dappled valleys of China, called him home, who shall blame him for lingering awhile amid his forest dreams with his fishing and the chase.

Yet solitude and the picturesque cannot hold him for long, nor even the ardours of the chase. Po Chü-i is above all the poet of human love and sorrow, and beyond all the consoler. Those who profess to find pessimism in the Chinese character must leave him alone. At the end of the great tragedy of 'The Never-ending Wrong' a whispered message of hope is borne to the lonely soul beating against the confines of the visible world:

'Tell my lord,' she murmured, 'to be firm of heart as this gold and enamel; then in heaven or earth below we twain may meet once more.'

It is the doctrine of eternal constancy, so dimly understood in the Western world, which bids the young wife immolate herself on her husband's tomb rather than marry again, and makes the whole world seem too small for the stricken Emperor with all the youth and beauty of China to command.

Po Chü-i

THE LUTE GIRL

The following is Po Chü-i's own preface to his poem:

When, after ten years of regular service, I was wrongfully dismissed from the Prefecture of the Nine Rivers and the Mastership of the Horse, in the bright autumn of the year I was sent away to Ko-pen Creek's mouth. It was there that I heard, seated in my boat at midnight, the faint tones of a lute. It seemed as though I was listening to the tones of the gongs in the Palace of the Capital. On asking an old man, I learnt that it was the performance of a woman who for many years had cultivated the two talents of music and singing to good effect. In the course of time her beauty faded, she humbled her pride, and followed her fate by becoming a merchant's wife.

. . . . . .

The wine ran out and the songs ceased. My grief was such that I made a few short poems to set to music for singing.

. . . . . .

But now perturbed, engulfed, distressed, worn out, I move about the river and lake at my leisure. I have been out of office for two years, but the effect of this man's words is such as to produce a peaceful influence within me.

This evening I feel that I have dismissed all the reproachful thoughts I harboured, and in consequence have made a long poem which I intend to present to the court.

By night, beside the river, underneath
The flower-like maple leaves that bloom alone
In autumn's silent revels of decay,
We said farewell. The host, dismounting, sped
The parting guest whose boat rocked under him,
And when the circling stirrup-cup went round,
No light guitar, no lute, was heard again;
But on the heart aglow with wine there fell
Beneath the cold bright moon the cold adieu
Of fading friends—when suddenly beyond

The Lute Girl

The cradled waters stole the lullaby
Of some faint lute; then host forgot to go,
Guest lingered on: all, wondering at the spell,
Besought the dim enchantress to reveal
Her presence; but the music died and gave
No answer, dying. Then a boat shot forth
To bring the shy musician to the shore.
Cups were refilled and lanterns trimmed again,
And so the festival went on. At last,
Slow yielding to their prayers, the stranger came,
Hiding her burning face behind her lute;
And twice her hand essayed the strings, and twice
She faltered in her task; then tenderly,
As for an old sad tale of hopeless years,
With drooping head and fingers deft she poured
Her soul forth into melodies. Now slow
The plectrum led to prayer the cloistered chords,
Now loudly with the crash of falling rain,
Now soft as the leaf whispering of words,
Now loud and soft together as the long
Patter of pearls and seed-pearls on a dish
Of marble; liquid now as from the bush
Warbles the mango bird; meandering
Now as the streamlet seawards; voiceless now
As the wild torrent in the strangling arms
Of her ice-lover, lying motionless,
Lulled in a passion far too deep for sound.
Then as the water from the broken vase
Gushes, or on the mailèd horseman falls
The anvil din of steel, as on the silk

The slash of rending, so upon the strings
Her plectrum fell. . . .
                              Then silence over us.
No sound broke the charmed air. The autumn moon
Swam silver o'er the tide, as with a sigh
The stranger stirred to go.
                              'I passed,' said she,
'My childhood in the capital; my home
Was near the hills. A girl of twelve, I learnt
The magic of the lute, the passionate
Blending of lute and voice that drew the souls
Of the great masters to acknowledgment;
And lovely women, envious of my face,
Bowed at the shrine in secret. The young lords
Vied for a look's approval. One brief song
Brought many costly bales. Gold ornaments
And silver pins were smashed and trodden down,
And blood-red silken skirts were stained with wine
In oft-times echoing applause. And so
I laughed my life away from year to year
While the spring breezes and the autumn moon
Caressed my careless head. Then on a day
My brother sought the battles in Kansuh;
My mother died: nights passed and mornings came,
And with them waned my beauty. Now no more
My doors were thronged; few were the cavaliers
That lingered by my side; so I became
A trader's wife, the chattel of a slave
Whose lord was gold, who, parting, little recked
Of separation and the unhonoured bride.

The Lute Girl

Since the tenth moon was full my husband went
To where the tea-fields ripen. I remained,
To wander in my little lonely boat
Over the cold bright wave o' nights, and dream
Of the dead days, the haze of happy days,
And see them set again in dreams and tears.'

. . . . . .

Already the sweet sorrows of her lute
Had moved my soul to pity; now these words
Pierced me the heart. 'Ah! lute-player,' said I,
'We are the vagrants of the world, and need
No ceremony to be friends. Last year
I left the Imperial City, banished far
To this plague-stricken spot, where desolation
Broods on from year to heavy year, nor lute
Nor love's guitar is heard. By marshy bank
Girt with tall yellow reeds and dwarf bamboos
I dwell. Night long and day no stir, no sound,
Only the lurking cuckoo's blood-stained note,
The gibbon's mournful wail. Hill songs I have,
And village pipes with their discordant twang.
But now I listen to thy lute methinks
The gods were parents to thy music. Sit
And sing to us again, while I engrave
Thy story on my tablets!' Gratefully
(For long she had been standing) the lute girl
Sat down and passed into another song,
Sad and so soft, a dream, unlike the song
Of now ago. Then all her hearers wept
In sorrow unrestrained; and I the more,

Po Chü-i

Weeping until the pale chrysanthemums
Upon my darkened robe were starred with dew.

❦ ❦

THE NEVER-ENDING WRONG

I have already alluded to the story of the Emperor Ming Huang
and the lady Yang Kwei-fei, or T'ai Chên, as she is called, in
my introduction. In order that the events which led up to her
tragic death may be understood, I have given in front of the
poem a short extract from the old Chinese annals translated into
French by the Jesuit Father Joseph de Mailla in 1778. The
Emperor is fleeing with a small, ill-disciplined force before the
rebellious general An Lu-shan into the province of Ssŭch'uan.
So the bald narrative resumes:

*As the Emperor was followed by a numerous suite, and because time
was lacking, the arrangements for so long a journey were found to be
insufficient. On their arrival at Ma-wei both officers and men murmured
loudly against Yang Kuochung,[1] accusing him of having brought all the
present evils upon them. The ambassador of the King of Tibet, followed
by twenty retainers, seeing the Prime Minister pass, stopped him, and
asked for provisions. Then the soldiers cried out that Yang was con-
spiring with the strangers, and throwing themselves upon him, they cut
off his head, which they exposed on a stake to the public gaze. The
Emperor, becoming aware of this violence, did not, however, dare to
exact punishment. He sent an officer to the chief of those who had slain
the Prime Minister, to find out the reason for their deed; he replied that
they had done so because Yang was on the point of rebellion. The leader
of the revolt even demanded the instant execution of the lady T'ai Chên,
as she was the sister of the supposed rebel, Yang. The Emperor, who
loved her, desired to prove her innocence by showing that it was impossible
for her, living always as she did within the Palace precincts, to be
confederate to her brother's plot. His envoy, however, urged him that
it was politic, after the events he had witnessed, to sacrifice her, innocent
as she was, if he wished to escape from the dangers of (another) revolu-*

[1] Minister of State, brother of T'ai Chên.

tion. The Emperor, yielding to political necessity, gave her into the hands of the envoy with the order that she should be strangled.

Ennui

Tired of pale languors and the painted smile,
His Majesty the Son of Heaven, long time
A slave of beauty, ardently desired
The glance that brings an Empire's overthrow.

Beauty

From the Yang family a maiden came,
Glowing to womanhood a rose aflame,
Reared in the inner sanctuary apart,
Lost to the world, resistless to the heart;
For beauty such as hers was hard to hide,
And so, when summoned to the monarch's side,
Her flashing eye and merry laugh had power
To charm into pure gold the leaden hour;
And through the paint and powder of the court
All gathered to the sunshine that she brought.
In spring, by the Imperial command,
The waters of Hua'ch'ing beheld her stand,
Laving her body in the crystal wave
Whose dimpled fount a warmth perennial gave.
Then when, her girls attending, forth she came,
A reed in motion and a rose in flame,
An empire passed into a maid's control,
And with her eyes she won a monarch's soul.

Revelry

Hair of cloud o'er face of flower,

Po Chü-i

Nodding plumes where she alights,
In the white hibiscus bower
She lingers through the soft spring nights—
Nights too short, though wearing late
Till the mimosa days are born.
Never more affairs of State
Wake them in the early morn.
Wine-stained moments on the wing,
Moonlit hours go luting by,
She who leads the flight of Spring
Leads the midnight revelry.
Flawless beauties, thousands three,
Deck the Imperial harem,[1]
Yet the monarch's eyes may see
Only one, and one supreme.
Goddess in a golden hall,
Fairest maids around her gleam,
Wine-fumes of the festival
Daily waft her into dream.
Smiles she, and her sires are lords,
Noble rank her brothers win:
Ah, the ominous awards
Showered upon her kith and kin!
For throughout the land there runs
Thought of peril, thought of fire;
Men rejoice not in their sons—
Daughters are their sole desire.
In the gorgeous palaces,
Piercing the grey skies above,

[1] Pronounced *hareem*.

Music on the languid breeze
Draws the dreaming world to love.
Song and dance and hands that sway
The passion of a thousand lyres
Ever through the live-long day,
And the monarch never tires.
Sudden comes the answer curt,
Loud the fish-skin war-drums roar;
Cease the plaintive 'rainbow skirt':
Death is drumming at the door.

Flight

Clouds upon clouds of dust enveloping
The lofty gates of the proud capital.
On, on, to the south-west, a living wall,
Ten thousand battle-chariots on the wing.

Feathers and jewels flashing through the crowd
Onwards, and then an halt. The legions wait
A hundred li beyond the western gate;
The great walls loom behind them wrapt in cloud.

No further stirs the sullen soldiery,
Naught but the last dread office can avail,
Till she of the dark moth-eyebrows, lily pale,
Shines through tall avenues of spears to die.

Upon the ground lie ornaments of gold,
One with the dust, and none to gather them,
Hair-pins of jade and many a costly gem,
Kingfishers' wings and golden birds scarce cold.

Po Chü-i

The king has sought the darkness of his hands,
Veiling the eyes that looked for help in vain,
And as he turns to gaze upon the slain,
His tears, her blood, are mingled on the sands

Exile

Across great plains of yellow sand,
    Where the whistling winds are blown,
Over the cloud-topped mountain peaks,
    They wend their way alone.

Few are the pilgrims that attain
    Mount Omi's heights afar;
And the bright gleam of their standard grows
    Faint as the last pale star.

Dark the Ssŭch'uan waters loom,
    Dark the Ssŭch'uan hills,
And day and night the monarch's life
    An endless sorrow fills.

The brightness of the foreign moon
    Saddens his lonely heart;
And a sound of a bell in the evening rain
    Doth rend his soul apart.

Return

The days go by, and once again,
Among the shadows of his pain,
He lingers at the well-known place
That holds the memory of her face.

But from the clouds of earth that lie
Beneath the foot of tall Ma-wei
No signs of her dim form appear,
Only the place of death is here.

Statesman's and monarch's eyes have met,
And royal robes with tears are wet;
Then eastward flies the frantic steed
As on to the Red Wall they speed.

Home

There is the pool, the flowers as of old,
There the hibiscus at the gates of gold,
And there the willows round the palace rise.
In the hibiscus flower he sees her face,
Her eyebrows in the willow he can trace,
And silken pansies thrill him with her eyes.

How in this presence should his tears not come,
In spring amid the bloom of peach and plum,
In autumn rains when the wut'ung leaves must fall?
South of the western palace many trees
Shower their dead leaves upon the terraces,
And not a hand to stir their crimson pall.

Ye minstrels of the Garden of the Pear,[1]
Grief with the touch of age has blanched your hair.
Ye guardians of the Pepper Chamber,[2] now

[1] The Pear Garden was a college of music founded by Ming Huang
for the purpose of training the youth of both sexes.
[2] The women's part of the palace.

Po Chü-i

No longer young to him, the firefly flits
Through the black hall where, lost to love, he sits,
Folding the veil of sorrows round his brow,

Alone, and one by one the lanterns die,
Sleep with the lily hands has passed him by,
Slowly the watches of the night are gone,
For now, alas! the nights are all too long,
And shine the stars, a silver, mocking throng,
As though the dawn were dead or slumbered on.

Cold settles on the painted duck and drake,
The frost a ghostly tapestry doth make,
Chill the kingfisher's quilt with none to share.
Parted by life and death; the ebb and flow
Of night and day over his spirit go;
He hunts her face in dreams, and finds despair.

Spirit-Land

A priest of Tao, one of the Hung-tu school,
Was able by his magic to compel
The spirits of the dead. So to relieve
The sorrows of his king, the man of Tao
Receives an urgent summons. Borne aloft
Upon the clouds, on ether charioted,
He flies with speed of lightning. High to heaven,
Low down to earth, he, seeking everywhere,
Floats on the far empyrean, and below
The yellow springs; but nowhere in great space
Can he find aught of her. At length he hears

An old-world tale: an Island of the Blest[1]—
So runs the legend—in mid-ocean lies
In realms of blue vacuity, too faint
To be descried; there gaily coloured towers
Rise up like rainbow clouds, and many gentle
And beautiful Immortals pass their days
In peace. Among them there is one whose name
Sounds upon lips as Eternal. By the bloom
Of her white skin and flower-like face he knows
That this is she. Knocking at the jade door
At the western gate of the golden house, he bids
A fair maid breathe his name to one more fair
Than all. She, hearing of this embassy
Sent by the Son of Heaven, starts from her dreams
Among the tapestry curtains. Gathering
Her robes around her, letting the pillow fall,
She, risen in haste, begins to deck herself
With pearls and gems. Her cloud-like hair, dishevelled,
Betrays the nearness of her sleep. And with the droop
Of her flowery plumes in disarray, she floats
Light through the hall. The sleeves of her divine
Raiment the breezes fill. As once again
To the Rainbow Skirt and Feather Jacket air
She seems to dance, her face is fixed and calm,
Though many tear-drops on an almond bough
Fall, and recall the rains of spring. Subdued
Her wild emotions and restrained her grief,
She tenders thanks unto his Majesty,
Saying how since they parted she had missed

[1] The fabled Island of P'eng-lai.

His form and voice; how, though their love had
   reached
Too soon its earthly limit, yet among
The blest a multitude of mellow noons
Remain ungathered. Turning now, she leans
Toward the land of the living, and in vain
Would find the Imperial city, lost in the dust
And haze. Then raising from their lacquered gloom
Old keepsakes, tokens of undying love,
A golden hair-pin, an enamel brooch,
She bids him bear them to her lord. One-half
The hair-pin still she keeps, one-half the brooch,
Breaking with her dim hands the yellow gold,
Sundering the enamel. 'Tell my lord,'
She murmured, 'to be firm of heart as this
Gold and enamel; then, in heaven or earth,
Below, we twain may meet once more.' At parting
She gave a thousand messages of love,
Among the rest recalled a mutual pledge,
How on the seventh day of the seventh moon,
Within the Hall of Immortality
At midnight, whispering, when none were near,
Low in her ear, he breathed, 'I swear that we,
Like to the one-winged birds, will ever fly,
Or grow united as the tree whose boughs
Are interwoven. Heaven and earth shall fall,
Long lasting as they are. But this great wrong
Shall stretch from end to end the universe,
And shine beyond the ruin of the stars.'

THE RIVER AND THE LEAF

Into the night the sounds of luting flow;
The west wind stirs amid the root-crop blue;
While envious fireflies spoil the twinkling dew,
And early wild-geese stem the dark Kin-ho.

Now great trees tell their secrets to the sky,
And hill on hill looms in the moon-clear night.
I watch one leaf upon the river light,
And in a dream go drifting down the Hwai.

❧ ❧

LAKE SHANG

Oh! she is like a picture in the spring,
This lake of Shang, with the wild hills gathering
Into a winding garden at the base
Of stormless waters; pines, deep blue, enlace
The lessening slopes, and broken moonlight gleams
Across the waves like pearls we thread in dreams.
Like a woof of jasper strands the corn unfolds,
Field upon field beyond the quiet wolds;
The late-blown rush flaunts in the dusk serene
Her netted sash and slender skirt of green.
Sadly I turn my prow toward the shore,
The dream behind me and the world before.
O Lake of Shang, his feet may wander far
Whose soul thou holdest mirrored as a star.

Po Chü-i

THE RUINED HOME

Who was the far-off founder of the house,
With its red gates abutting to the road?—
A palace, though its outer wings are shorn,
And domes of glittering tiles. The wall without
Has tottered into ruin, yet remain
The straggling fragments of some seven courts,
The wreck of seven fortunes: roof and eaves
Still hang together. From this chamber cool
The dense blue smoke arose. Nor heat nor cold
Now dwells therein. A tall pavilion stands
Empty beside the empty rooms that face
The pine-browed southern hills. Long purple vines
Frame the verandahs.

            Mount the sunken step
Of the red, joyous threshold, and shake down
The peach and cherry branches. Yonder group
Of scarlet peonies hath ringed about
A lordly fellow with ten witnesses
Of his official rank. The taint of meat
Lingers around the kitchen, and a trace
Of vanished hoards the treasury retains.

  .   .   .   .   .   .

Who can lay hold upon my words? Give heed
And commune with thyself! How poor and mean
Is the last state of wretchedness, when cold
And famine thunder at the gates, and none
But pale endurance on the threshold stands
With helpless hands and hollow eyes, the dumb

Beholder of calamity. O thou
That would protect the land a thousand years,
Behold they are not that herein once bloomed
And perished; but the garden breathes of them,
And all the flowers are fragrant for their sakes.
Salute the garden that salutes the dead!

❀ ❀

A PALACE STORY

A network handkerchief contains no tear.
'Tis dawn at court ere wine and music sate.
The rich red crops no aftermath await.
Rest on a screen, and you will fall, I fear.

❀ ❀

PEACEFUL OLD AGE

Chuang Tzŭ said: 'Tao[1] gives me this toil in manhood, this repose in old age, this rest in death."

Swiftly and soon the golden sun goes down,
The blue sky wells afar into the night.
Tao is the changeful world's environment;
Happy are they that in its laws delight.

Tao gives me toil, youth's passion to achieve,
And leisure in life's autumn and decay.
I follow Tao—the seasons are my friends;
Opposing it misfortunes come my way.

[1] Literally, 'The Way'.

Po Chü-i

Within my breast no sorrows can abide;
I feel the great world's spirit through me thrill,
And as a cloud I drift before the wind,
Or with the random swallow take my will.

As underneath the mulberry-tree I dream,
The water-clock drips on, and dawn appears:
A new day shines on wrinkles and white hair,
The symbols of the fulness of my years.

If I depart, I cast no look behind:
Still wed to life, I still am free from care.
Since life and death in cycles come and go,
Of little moment are the days to spare.

Thus strong in faith I wait, and long to be
One with the pulsings of Eternity.

❀ ❀

SLEEPLESSNESS

I cannot rest when the cool is gone from June,
But haunt the dim verandah till the moon
      Fades from the dawn's pursuit.
The stirrup-fires beneath the terrace flare;
Over the star-domed court a low, sad air
      Roams from a hidden lute.

This endless heat doth urge me to extremes;
Yet cool of autumn waits till the wild goose screams

In the track of whirling skies.
My hand is laid upon the cup once more,
And of the red-gold vintage I implore
  The sleep that night denies.

❀❀ ❀❀

THE GRASS

How beautiful and fresh the grass returns!
When golden days decline, the meadow burns;
Yet autumn suns no hidden root have slain,
The spring winds blow, and there is grass again.

Green rioting on olden ways it falls:
The blue sky storms the ruined city walls;
Yet since Wang Sun departed long ago,
When the grass blooms both joy and fear I know.

❀❀ ❀❀

AUTUMN ACROSS THE FRONTIER

The last red leaves droop sadly o'er the slain;
In the long tower my cup of wine I drain,
Watching the mist-flocks driven through the hills,
And great blown roses ravished by the rain.

The beach tints linger down the frontier line,
And sounding waters shimmer to the brine;
Over the Yellow Kingdom breaks the sun,
Yet dreams, and woodlands, and the chase are mine.

Po Chü-i

THE FLOWER FAIR

The city walls rise up to greet
    Spring's luminous twilight hours;
The clamour of carts goes down the street:
    This is the Fair of Flowers.
Leisure and pleasure drift along,
Beggar and marquis join the throng,
And care, humility, rank, and pride
In the sight of the flowers are laid aside.
Bright, oh! bright are a thousand shades,
Crimson splashes and slender blades
    With five white fillets bound.
Tents are here that will cover all,
Ringed with trellis and leafy wall,
    And the dust is laid around.
Naught but life doth here display;
The dying flower is cast away;
Families meet and intermingle,
Lovers are parted, and friends go single.
    One ambition all avow—
A roof to harbour, a field to plough.
See, they come to the Flower Fair,
Youth and maiden, a laughing pair.
Bowed and sighing the greybeard wends
Alone to the mart where sighing ends.
For here is a burden all may bear,
The crimson and gold of the Flower Fair.

THE PENALTIES OF RANK

Three score and ten! A slave to office yet!
In the Li Chi these luminous words befall:
'The lust for honours honours not at all,'
Here is the golden line we most forget.

Alas! how these long years afflict a man!
When teeth are gone, and failing eyes grow dim.
The morning dews brought dreams of fame to him
Who bears in dusk the burdens of his clan.

His eyes still linger on the tassel blue,
And still the red sedan of rank appeals,
But his shrunk belly scarce the girdle feels
As, bowed, he crawls the Prince's Gateway through.

Where is the man that would not wealth acclaim?
Who would not truckle for his sovereign's grace?
Yet years of high renown their furrows trace,
And greatness overwhelms the weary frame.

The springs of laughter flow not from his heart,
Where bide the dust and glamour of old days.
Who walks alone in contemplation's ways?
'Tis he, the happy man, who dwells apart.

❦ ❦

THE ISLAND OF PINES

Across the willow-lake a temple shines,
Pale, through the lotus-girdled isle of pines,

And twilight listens to the drip of oars—
The coming of dark boats with scented stores
Of orange seed; the mist leans from the hill,
While palm leaves sway 'twixt wind and water chill,
And waves of smoke like phantoms rise and fade
Into a trembling tangle of green jade.
I dream strange dreams within my tower room,
Dreams from the glimmering realms of even gloom;
Until each princely guest doth, landing, raise
His eyes, upon the full-orbed moon to gaze—
The old moon-palace that in ocean stands
Mid clouds of thistle-down and jewelled strands.

SPRINGTIDE

The lonely convent on the hill
Draws merchants faring from the west:
Almost upon the waters still
The quiet clouds lean down and rest.
In green pavilions of warm trees
The golden builders toil and sing;
While swallows dip along the leas,
And dabble in the ooze of Spring.

A thousand flowers, a thousand dreams,
Bright pageants in confusion pass.
See yonder, where the white horse gleams
His fetlocks deep in pliant grass.

Beside the eastern lake there calls
No laughing throng, no lover goes;
But in the long embankment walls
The willow shade invites repose.

❦ ❦

THE ANCIENT WIND

The peach blooms open on the eastern wall—
I breathe their fragrance, laughing in the glow
Of golden noontide. Suddenly there comes
The revelation of the ancient wind,
Flooding my soul with glory; till I feel
One with the brightness of the first far dawn,
One with the many-coloured spring; and all
The secrets of the scented hearts of flowers
Are whispered through me; till I cry aloud:—
'Alas! how grey and scentless is the bloom
Of mortal life!' This—this alone I fear,
That from yon twinkling mirror of delight
The unreal flowers may fade; that with the breath
Of the fiery flying Dragon they will fall
Petal by petal, slowly, yet too soon,
Into the world's green sepulchre. Alas!
My little friends, my lovers, we must part,
And, like some uncompanioned pine that stands,
Last of the legions on the southern slopes,
I too shall stand alone, and hungry winds
Shall gnaw the lute-strings of my desolate heart.

Li Hua

CIRCA A.D. 850

❀ ❀

AN OLD BATTLE-FIELD

Vast, vast—an endless wilderness of sand;
A stream crawls through its tawny banks; the hills
Encompass it; where in the dismal dusk
Moan the last sighs of sunset. Shrubs are gone,
Withered the grass; all chill as the white rime
Of early morn. The birds go soaring past,
The beasts avoid it; for the legend runs—
Told by the crook'd custodian of the place—
Of some old battle-field. 'Here many a time,'
He quavered, 'armies have been overwhelmed,
And the faint voices of the unresting dead
Often upon the darkness of the night
Go wailing by.'

        O sorrow! O ye Ch'ins!
Ye Hans! ye dynasties for ever flown!
Ye empires of the dust! for I have heard
How, when the Ch'is and Weis embattled rose
Along the frontier, when the Chings and Hans

An Old Battle-field

Gathered their multitudes, a myriad leagues
Of utter weariness they trod. By day
Grazing their jaded steeds, by night they ford
The hostile stream. The endless earth below,
The boundless sky above, they know no day
Of their return. Their breasts are ever bared
To the pitiless steel and all the wounds of war
Unspeakable.

       Methinks I see them now,
Dust-mantled in the bitter wind, a host
Of Tartar warriors in ambuscade.
Our leader scorns the foe. He would give battle
Upon the threshold of the camp. The stream
Besets a grim array where order reigns,
Though many hearts may beat, where discipline
Is all, and life of no account.

       The spear
Now works its iron will, the startled sand
Blinding the combatants together locked
In the death-grip; while hill and vale and stream
Glow with the flash and crash of arms. Then cold
The shades of night o'erwhelm them; to the knee
In snow, beards stiff with ice. The carrion bird
Hath sought its nest. The war-horse in its strength
Is broken. Clothes avail not. Hands are dead,
Flesh to the frost succumbs. Nature herself
Doth aid the Tartar with a deadly blast
Following the wild onslaught. Wagons block
The way. Our men, beset with flank attacks,
Surrender with their officers. Their chief

Li Hua

Is slain. The river to its topmost banks
Swollen with death; the dykes of the Great Wall
Brimming with blood. Nation and rank are lost
In that vast-heaped corruption.

                      Faintly now,
And fainter beats the drum; for strength is shorn,
And arrows spent, and bow-strings snapped, and
    swords
Shattered. The legions fall on one another
In the last surge of life and death. To yield
Is to become a slave; to fight is but
To mingle with the desert sands.

.   .   .   .   .   .   No sound
Of bird now flutters from the hushed hillside;
All, all is still, save for the wind that wails
And whistles through the long night where the ghosts
Hither and thither in the gloom go by,
And spirits from the nether world arise
Under the ominous clouds. The sunlight pales
Athwart the trampled grass; the fading moon
Still twinkles on the frost-flakes scattered round.

Ssü-K'ung T'u

A.D. 834–908

Little is known of his life, except that he was Secretary to the Board of Rites and retired from this position to lead the contemplative life. His introduction to the European world is entirely due to Professor Giles. No mention is made of him in the French collection of the T'ang poets by the Marquis de Saint-Denys. Yet the importance of his work cannot well be over-estimated. He is perhaps the most Chinese of the poets dealt with, and certainly one of the most philosophical. By his subtly simple method of treatment, lofty themes are clothed in the bright raiment of poetry. If through the red pine woods, or amid the torrent of peach-blossom rushing down the valley, some mortal beauty strays, she is but a symbol, a lure that leads us by way of the particular into the universal. Whatever senses we possess may be used as means of escape from the prison of personality into the boundless freedom of the spiritual world. And once the soul is set free, there is no need for painful aimless wanderings, no need for Mahomet to go to the Mountain, for resting in the centre of all things the universe will be our home and our share in the secrets of the World-Builder will be made known.

> Freighted with eternal principles
> Athwart the night's void,
> Where cloud masses darken,
> And the wind blows ceaseless around,
> Beyond the range of conceptions
> Let us gain the Centre,

> And there hold fast without violence,
> Fed from an inexhaustible supply.[1]

With such a philosophy there are infinite possibilities. The poet is an occultist in the truest sense of the word. For him, Time and Space no longer exist, and by 'concentration' he is able to communicate with the beloved, and

> Sweet words falter to and fro—
> Though the great River rolls between.

Ssü-K'ung T'u, more than any poet, teaches how unreal are the apparent limitations of man. 'He is the peer of heaven and earth': 'A co-worker in Divine transformation'. With his keen vision the poet sees things in a glance and paints them in a single line, and in the poem as a whole you get the sense of beauty beyond beauty, as though the seer had looked into a world that underlay the world of form. And yet there is nothing strained, no peering through telescopes to find new worlds or magnify the old; the eyes need only be lifted for a moment, and the great power is not the power of sight, but sympathy.

And Nature, ever prodigal to her lovers, repays their favours in full measure. To this old artist-lover she grants no petty details, no chance revelations of this or that sweetness and quality but her whole pure self. Yet such a gift is illimitable; he may only win from secret to secret and die unsatisfied.

> You grasp ten thousand, and secure one.

This might well be written over his tomb, if any verse were needed to encompass him. By entering into harmony with his environment, Ssü-K'ung T'u allowed his splendid vitality to find expression, and after the lapse of a thousand years these glowing pages torn from the book of life have drifted towards us like rose-leaves down a sombre stream.

[1] *Chinese Literature*, p. 179.

RETURN OF SPRING

A lovely maiden, roaming
  The wild dark valley through,
Culls from the shining waters
  Lilies and lotus blue.
With leaves the peach-trees are laden,
  The wind sighs through the haze,
And the willows wave their shadows
  Down the oriole-haunted ways.
As, passion-tranced, I follow,
  I hear the old refrain
Of Spring's eternal story,
  That was old and is young again.

❧ ❧

THE COLOUR OF LIFE

Would that we might for ever stay
The rainbow glories of the world,
The blue of the unfathomed sea,
The rare azalea late unfurled,
The parrot of a greener spring,
The willows and the terrace line,
The stranger from the night-steeped hills,
The roselit brimming cup of wine.
Oh for a life that stretched afar,
Where no dead dust of books were rife,
Where spring sang clear from star to star;
Alas! what hope for such a life?

Ssŭ-K'ung T'u

SET FREE

I revel in flowers without let,
An atom at random in space;
My soul dwells in regions ethereal,
And the world is my dreaming-place.

As the tops of the ocean I tower,
As the winds of the air spreading wide,
I am 'stablished in might and dominion and power,
With the universe ranged at my side.

Before me the sun, moon, and stars,
Behind me the phœnix doth clang;
In the morning I lash my leviathans,
And I bathe my feet in Fusang.

❧ ❧

FASCINATION

Fair is the pine grove and the mountain stream
That gathers to the valley far below,
The black-winged junks on the dim sea reach, adream,
The pale blue firmament o'er banks of snow.
And her, more fair, more supple smooth than jade,
Gleaming among the dark red woods I follow:
Now lingering, now as a bird afraid
Of pirate wings she seeks the haven hollow.
Vague, and beyond the daylight of recall,
Into the cloudland past my spirit flies,

As though before the gold of autumn's fall,
Before the glow of the moon-flooded skies.

❈❈

TRANQUIL REPOSE

It dwells in the quiet silence,
    Unseen upon hill and plain,
'Tis lapped by the tideless harmonies,
    It soars with the lonely crane.

As the springtime breeze whose flutter
    The silken skirts hath blown,
As the wind-drawn note of the bamboo flute
    Whose charm we would make our own,—

Chance-met, it seems to surrender;
    Sought, and it lures us on;
Ever shifting in form and fantasy,
    It eludes us, and is gone.

❈❈

THE POET'S VISION

Wine that recalls the glow of spring,
Upon the thatch a sudden shower,
A gentle scholar in the bower,
Where tall bamboos their shadows fling,
White clouds in heavens newly clear,
And wandering wings through depths of trees,

Then pillowed in green shade, he sees
A torrent foaming to the mere;
Around his dreams the dead leaves fall;
Calm as the starred chrysanthemum,
He notes the season glories come,
And reads the books that never pall.

❧ ❧

DESPONDENT

A gale goes ruffling down the stream,
The giants of the forest crack;
My thoughts are bitter—black as death—
For she, my summer, comes not back.

A hundred years like water glide,
Riches and rank are ashen cold,
Daily the dream of peace recedes:
By whom shall Sorrow be consoled?

The soldier, dauntless, draws his sword,
And there are tears and endless pain;
The winds arise, leaves flutter down,
And through the old thatch drips the rain.

❧ ❧

EMBROIDERIES

If rank and wealth within the mind abide,
Then gilded dust is all your yellow gold.
Kings in their fretted palaces grow old;

Youth dwells for ever at Contentment's side.
A mist cloud hanging at the river's brim,
Pink almond flowers along the purple bough,
A hut rose-girdled under moon-swept skies,
A painted bridge half-seen in shadows dim,—
These are the splendours of the poor, and thou,
O wine of spring, the vintage of the wise.

❀ ❀

CONCENTRATION

A hut green-shadowed among firs,—
A sun that slopes in amber air,—
Lone wandering, my head I bare,
While some far thrush the silence stirs.

No flocks of wild geese thither fly,
And she—ah! she is far away;
Yet all my thoughts behold her stay,
As in the golden hours gone by.
The clouds scarce dim the water's sheen,
The moon-bathed islands wanly show,
And sweet words falter to and fro—
Though the great River rolls between.

❀ ❀

MOTION

Like a water-wheel awhirl,
Like the rolling of a pearl;

Ssü-K'ung T'u

      Yet these but illustrate,
      To fools, the final state.
The earth's great axis spinning on,
The never-resting pole of sky—
Let us resolve their Whence and Why,
And blend with all things into One;
Beyond the bounds of thought and dream,
Circling the vasty void as spheres
Whose orbits round a thousand years:
Behold the Key that fits my theme.

Ou-yang Hsiu of Lu-ling

A.D. 1007–1072

With the completion of the T'ang dynasty, it was my design to bring this work to conclusion. I have, however, decided to include Ou-Yang Hsiu of the Sung dynasty, if only for the sake of his 'Autumn', which many competent critics hold to be one of the finest things in Chinese literature. His career was as varied as his talents. In collaboration with the historian Sung C'hi he prepared a history of the recent T'ang dynasty. He also held the important post of Grand Examiner, and was at one time appointed a Governor in the provinces. It is difficult to praise the 'Autumn' too highly. With its daring imagery, grave magnificence of language and solemn thought, it is nothing less than Elizabethan, and only the masters of that age could have done it justice in the rendering.

❀ ❀

AUTUMN

One night, when dreaming over ancient books,
There came to me a sudden far-off sound
From the south-west. I listened, wondering,
As on it crept: at first a gentle sigh,
Like as a spirit passing; then it swelled
Into the roaring of great waves that smite
The broken vanguard of the cliff: the rage
Of storm-black tigers in the startled night
Among the jackals of the wind and rain.

Ou-yang Hsiu of Lu-ling

It burst upon the hanging bell, and set
The silver pendants chattering. It seemed
A muffled march of soldiers hurriedly
Sped to the night attack with muffled mouths,
When no command is heard, only the tramp
Of men and horses onward. 'Boy,' said I,
What sound is that? Go forth and see.' My boy,
Returning, answered, 'Lord! the moon and all
Her stars shine fair; the silver river spans
The sky. No sound of man is heard without;
Tis but a whisper of the trees.' 'Alas!'
I cried, 'then Autumn is upon us now.
Tis thus, O boy, that Autumn comes, the cold
Pitiless autumn of the wrack and mist,
Autumn, the season of the cloudless sky,
Autumn, of biting blasts, the time of blight
And desolation; following the chill
Stir of disaster, with a shout it leaps
Upon us. All the gorgeous pageantry
Of green is changed. All the proud foliage
Of the crested forests is shorn, and shrivels down
Beneath the blade of ice. For this is Autumn,
Nature's chief executioner. It takes
The darkness for a symbol. It assumes
The temper of proven steel. Its symbol is
A sharpened sword. The avenging fiend, it rides
Upon an atmosphere of death. As Spring,
Mother of many-coloured birth, doth rear
The young light-hearted world, so Autumn drains
The nectar of the world's maturity.

And sad the hour when all ripe things must pass,
For sweetness and decay are of one stem
And sweetness ever riots to decay.
Still, what availeth it? The trees will fall
In their due season. Sorrow cannot keep
The plants from fading. Stay! there yet is man—
Man, the divinest of all things, whose heart
Hath known the shipwreck of a thousand hopes,
Who bears a hundred wrinkled tragedies
Upon the parchment of his brow, whose soul
Strange cares have lined and interlined, until
Beneath the burden of life his inmost self
Bows down. And swifter still he seeks decay
When groping for the unattainable
Or grieving over continents unknown.
Then come the snows of time. Are they not due?
Is man of adamant he should outlast
The giants of the grove? Yet after all
Who is it saps his strength save man alone?
Tell me, O boy, by what imagined right
Man doth accuse his Autumn blast?' My boy
Slumbered and answered not. The cricket gave
The only answer to my song of death.

❀ ❀

AT THE GRAVESIDE

Years since we last foregathered, O Man-ch'ing!
     Methinks I see thee now,
     Lord of the noble brow,
And courage from thy glances challenging.

Ou-yang Hsiu of Lu-ling

Ah! when thy tired limbs were fain to keep
    The purple cerements of sleep,
        Thy dim beloved form
        Passed from the sunshine warm,
From the corrupting earth, that sought to hold
Its beauty, to the essence of pure gold.
Or haply art thou some far-towering pine,—
        Some rare and wondrous flower?
        What boots it, this sad hour?
Here in thy loneliness the eglantine
Weaves her sweet tapestries above thy head,
        While blow across thy bed,
Moist with the dew of heaven, the breezes chill:
Fire-fly, will-o'-the-wisp, and wandering star
Glow in thy gloom, and naught is heard but the far
Chanting of woodman and shepherd from the hill,
        Naught but the startled bird is seen
        Soaring away in the moonland sheen,
Or the hulk of the scampering beast that fears
        Their plaintive lays as, to and fro,
        The pallid singers go.
Such is thy loneliness. A thousand years,
Haply ten thousand, hence the fox shall make
His fastness in thy tomb, the weasel take
Her young to thy dim sanctuary. Such is the lot
        For ever of the great and wise,
        Whose tombs around us rise;
Man honours where the grave remembers not.
        Ah! that a song could bring
        Peace to thy dust, Man-ch'ing!

Bibliography

Since the first edition of this book was published there have been innumerable translations from Chinese classical poetry in English, French and German. A more up-to-date bibliography is essential, though it is not the author's intention to refer to every paraphrase, translation or free rendering, but rather to give the reader a brief list of the more important works that have appeared in recent years. If no mention of the *Shih Ching* or Book of Odes collected by Confucius is made it is because, in his opinion, the older translations of Legge, Allen, Jennings and Couvreur are out of date and there is nothing to take their place. Miss Helen Waddell's 'Lyrics from the Chinese' is a charming little collection of 36 out of 312 poems, an apéritif to a banquet not yet provided.

GENERAL COLLECTIONS OF CHINESE CLASSICAL POETRY

AYSCOUGH, FLORENCE, and LOWELL, AMY
Fir-Flower Tablets. (Constable)

BYNNER, WITTER, and KIANG KANG-HU
The Jade Mountain. (Alfred Knopf)

FLETCHER, W. J. B.
Gems of Chinese Poetry.
More Gems of Chinese Poetry. (Shanghai)

HART, HENRY H.
A Chinese Market. (Peking)
The Hundred Names. (Cambridge University Press)

HAWKES, DAVID
Ch'u Tz'u: The Songs of the South. (Oxford University Press, 1958)

Bibliography

JOERISSEN, GERTRUDE
    The Lost Flute. (Fisher Unwin)

WALEY, ARTHUR
    170 Chinese Poems. (Constable)
    More Translations from the Chinese. (Allen & Unwin)
    The Temple, and other Poems. (Allen & Unwin)

SUNG DYNASTY POETS

A.D. 906–1278

CANDLIN, CLARA M.
    The Herald Wind, Translations of Sung Dynasty.
    Poems, Lyrics and Songs. (John Murray)

SOULIÉ DE MORANT, GEORGE
    Florilège des poèmes Song. (Paris)

INDIVIDUAL POETS

OBATA SHIGEYOSHI
    The Works of Li-Po. (Dent)

AYSCOUGH, FLORENCE
    Tu Fu, The Autobiography of a Chinese Poet. (Cape)
    Travels of a Chinese Poet. (Cape)

LE GROS CLARK, CYRIL DRUMMOND
    Selections from the Works of Su Tung-P'o. (Cape)